JOSEPH HARDMAN
LAKELAND PHOTOGRAPHER
1893-1972

With acknowledgement to the assistance of the Curwen Archives Trust

Published by

HELM
PRESS

Dedicated to all the people who have enjoyed Joseph Hardman's
photographs over the years

Published by Helm Press
10 Abbey Gardens, Natland, Kendal. Cumbria LA9 7SP
Tel: 015395 61321

First published 2016

Typeset in Baskerville

ISBN 978 0 9550823 5 1

Typeset and printed by MTP Media Ltd

Front cover: Joseph standing with camera
(Courtesy of the Museum of Lakeland Life & Industry, Lakeland Arts)

Contents

Introduction

1. Early Years 1
2. First World War 7
3. Kendal, Marriage and Photography 13
4. Later Years 29
5. The People who Remember Joseph and Edith 37
  Eric Shaw – Nephew...37
  Michael Bottomley – Architect and Artist 39
  Mary Whitwell – Farmer's Wife..40
  Tommy Bland – Blacksmith and Volunteer Fireman 42
  Clara Black – Farmer's Wife 44
  Andrew Cannon...45
6. The Models 47
  Sylvia Deacon 49
  Delia Shaw 51
  Joyce Taylor..55
  Daphne Rockcliff 58
  Gwyneth Dillarstone 59
7. Digitising and bringing into the 21st Century............................65
8. The Re-enactment of the sheep coming down Allhallows
 Lane, Kendal 67
9. What a Picture!...69
10. Summing up Joseph's Legacy and the Future.............................101
  Sources 105

Glass plate negative (Cumbria Archive Centre, Kendal)

Eric Shaw, Joseph's nephew, with some of Joseph's camera equipment

Introduction

Joseph Hardman was a young man, who came from Lancashire to the Lake District looking for work with his brother, Walter in the early 1900s. They settled in Kendal and set up a window cleaning business and in his spare time he took up photography. From this low key beginning he produced at least 50-60,000 negatives (glass plates) together with his many wonderful black and white photographs of which, sadly, only a fraction now survive but give us none-the-less a lasting insight/legacy of mainly country life in the Lake District and beyond, for which we must be eternally grateful.

I first came across Joseph Hardman's photographs nearly twenty years ago when looking for suitable photographs with my late friend Fred Nevinson to illustrate his book 'A Westmorland Shepherd'. The manuscript was already at the printers when he found the old chocolate box he had been looking for containing photographs and newspaper cuttings. The ones I was drawn to were by Joseph Hardman. Fred told me they had been taken by the photographer who came to the farm by taxi and later on would be given a copy to keep. The Hardman photographs indeed stood out from the rest, they had that extra something. A few of these photographs were added to Fred's book and helped to illustrate it beautifully.

Hardman photographs are indeed a work of art – each shows the time and care taken by the artist he surely was, and every picture tells a story. Like a lot of things – had people only but known of their true significance and value (not in monetary terms) – greater care would have been taken to preserve them and many more may have still been around today.

I have tried to piece together what is known of this quiet gentleman, the people who knew him so that he can be remembered by future generations for the great artist/ photographer he surely was.

In the last few years his name and work have come to the fore and are being aired and appreciated for the great legacy he built up and left for all to see.

I would also like to thank some of the many people who helped to make this book possible, either by giving information, lending photographs and also encouragement along the way. Firstly, to Eric Shaw, Joseph's nephew, Margaret Reid, James Arnold, and Rachel Roberts at the Museum of Lakeland Life and Industry together with Peter Eyre and staff at Cumbria Archive Centre, Kendal. Also to Jackie Faye and Sylvia Kelly at the Local Studies Section in Kendal Library, and Chris Payne. Liz Stannard and Andrew Keogh at the Cumberland and Westmorland Herald; Dick and Pamela White who advised and encouraged me to keep going. Not forgetting my friend Maura Machin who has, over the years, proof read my work and made it readable. Also, to Patricia Hovey who helped me make that final step to publication. I hope you will enjoy learning a bit more about Joseph Hardman, Kendal's very own pictorial artist and press photographer, whom we should be justly proud.

Anne Bonney

Anne Bonney

October 2016

NB When interviewing the models and other people who knew Joseph Hardman – I have treated it as an item of Oral History and have written down or recorded what they actually said.

Chapter One

Early Years

Joseph Hardman was born on 21ˢᵗ January 1893, at 35 Ainsworth Road, Radcliffe, Manchester, in the County of Lancashire, and was one of five children. Radcliffe is situated seven miles north of Manchester. His mother - Elizabeth Hardman (nee Francis) is shown in the 1901 Census Record as being born in 1855 at Check O' Bent, Lancashire – the old name for part of Atherton, five miles from Wigan. His father, Walter Hardman, was a yeast dealer and would travel round the various bakers' and grocers' shops in the district. The Census shows that the family had moved next door to 33 Ainsworth Road, with only five people living there now, Elizabeth aged 46 years, widow and head of the household, together with daughter Ellen A., 24 years old, single, employed as a cotton winder; Walter, a son aged 12 years, employed as wash-house boy at a cotton mill, then Joseph, a son, 8 years old and lastly Mildred, daughter 5 years. They may have moved next door for economic reasons – less rent or just swapped with their neighbours. I later found a photograph of a gravestone

and this showed that Walter Hardman (their father) had died on 1st September 1895, in his 44th year and also Mildred, his daughter died 3rd August 1903, aged 8 years, also John Wallwork, son died 7th November 1889, aged 8 weeks. Another daughter, Martha, was still-born on 15th November 1879.

Like all children born in these times into working class mill families, life would be hard with long hours and the little money earned by the children would go to help pay the rent, food and other essentials. Things would be extra difficult without their father.

Lancashire was well known for its mill towns and thousands were employed here during the height of the Industrial Revolution. In the early 1900s Radcliffe had over sixty mills for manufacturing goods and fifteen spinning mills, plus eighteen which bleached, dyed, raised and finished every kind of cotton cloth.

The Britannia Shuttle Works (Francis Hill & Co Ltd) Ebury Street, in Radcliffe was close to where Joseph and his family lived and he worked there part-time whilst still at school – this was quite normal in these times. No doubt most of the mill workers lived nearby as they did in those days.

From an article in the Radcliffe Times, dated 6th January 1900 – under the heading 'Men still pooh-poohed power-looms' we learn that the mill supplied annually 300,000 shuttles by steam power to help provide the vast quantity required by the textile machine industry both in this country and perhaps the world. The factory employed between 80-100 men and boys. It goes on to mention the rarity of such works stating -

> *'It was a model workshop in every regard to health and safety. General cleanliness above that insisted by Her Majesty's Inspectors eg elaborate and expensive systems of fans by which the dust and refuse resulting from the works is drawn from each man's bench or work place and sucked into a metal tube, and then blown into a small chamber specially built for the purpose. Every modern appliance is used.'*

So perhaps it is not surprising that, owing to its location and its good name, we find that Joseph worked there as a 'half-timer' from eleven years old to help the family. One week he went to school in the mornings and worked in the afternoons; the next week vice versa. And at the end of his week of combined work and schooling he took home a pay packet containing precisely 1s 10d (9p) or 3s 4d (17p) according to whether he was at the factory in the afternoons or in the mornings of that particular week.

He left school at fourteen and began working full-time. A few years later, in 1911, Joseph and Walter, his older brother set out looking for other work and came to Kendal. Stories differ in that there was a strike at the firm or simply the lure of Kendal and the beautiful Lakes proved irresistible. The brothers formed 'The Kendal Window Cleaning Company' at Waterside near the centre of town. Walter, with a keen business eye, saw an opportunity later to expand into carpet cleaning after touting for business in the many Lake District hotels and acquired a carpet cleaning machine. We can assume that Walter was the major instigator of this as Joseph never learned to drive. So maybe Walter did this by himself.

Details of their advertisement in The Westmorland Gazette Directory of 1930:-

Kendal Window Cleaning Co.,
Waterside (W. Hardman. Proprietor Tel 495)

Walter obviously prospered, later married, and lived happily at Murley Moss – a large house and garden on the edge of town just off Oxenholme Road, where family and friends regularly used to meet.

Joseph in his early years had shown an artistic bent, but at that time his inclination was towards drawing. He was a quiet, unassuming young man who would go about his daily work in Kendal cleaning windows, carrying his steps or using his cycle to get around. He had plenty of time to think, quietly watching and observing people going about their daily work and cycling out into the countryside when time permitted. The brothers had bought a camera for £4 between them and Joseph bought out Walter's share as he became keener and joined the Kendal Photographic Society which was formed in 1910. We have no record of the exact date he joined and became a keen amateur photographer.

CARRIER: "Try zideways, Mrs. Jones, try zideways!"

MRS. JONES: "Lor' bless yer, John, I ain't got no zideways!"

A drawing by Joseph Hardman (Cumbria Archive Centre, Kendal)

4

Highgate, Kendal

Joseph in Uniform (Cumbria Archive Centre, Kendal)

3 Park Avenue, Kendal

Chapter Two

First World War

On 8th July 1918 Joseph bought No 3 Park Avenue, Kendal, a two-bedroomed terraced house, for £250. The Conveyance was signed by him whilst he was in Plymouth and his mother Elizabeth was living there to begin with.

Joseph was in the Royal Marines in the First World War. He was presumably called-up as he was not working in a reserved occupation. A photo-copy of his war service record showed the brief time he had served in the Marines before becoming injured and invalided out. He enlisted on 11th September 1917 at Liverpool into the Royal Marine Light Infantry Division Number 2493; religion – Wesleyan; next of kin - his mother Elizabeth at No 3 Park Avenue, Kendal. Description - fresh complexion, blue eyes, 5' 8 ½" though on discharge 5' 10 ¼" (which would be correct) and character 'very good'.

The details of his record given under the various headings are as follows:-
He was a private in 'A' Company at the Recruit Depot at Deal, from 11th September to 29th December 1917. He was then transferred to Plymouth to 'D' Division and was there from 30th December to 31st December – only two days. At Plymouth Division he was in the 4th (RMBD – Royal Marine Battalion Devonport) from 1st January 1918 to 23rd February 1918

In the brief training was listed – musketry on 1st December 1917, infantry on 28th December, field training on 29th December 1917 and building on 29th January 1918.

The next details we have are under the heading of wounds and hurts, special services etc and learn that, between 22nd and 25th April 1918, he took part in the attack on Zeebrugge.

On 25th April 1918 – hurt (injury) certificate granted. Shell wound left upper arm, left side of back, 2nd and 3rd fingers right hand in action.

After returning from Zeebrugge on 27th April he was discharged and invalided out on 29th November 1918. Signed E. J. Stroud (Dr). Mention of medal and gratuity and for RFR (Ready for release).

Much has been written of this attack – 'The Raid on Zeebrugge' and in great detail.

In August 1914 the Germans invaded Belgium giving their submarines direct access to the North Sea via Zeebrugge. They built heavily defended submarine pens inland at Bruges, out of range of the guns of the Royal Navy's battleships. The submarines travelled to the coast via the Zeebrugge and Ostend canals and on into the North Sea, the English Channel and the Atlantic. German submarines sank a huge amount of merchant shipping in an attempt to starve Britain out of the war.

Hence a grand plan was carefully thought out to try and block the exits from both ports thus denying the German submarines convenient bases. It was planned in great secrecy and in part conducted by a volunteer force. The main force of the attack was to be at Zeebrugge to block the entrance canal by filling cruisers HMS Intrepid, Thetis and Iphigenia with concrete and sinking them.

To prevent the Germans reinforcing their troops on the Mole (this was the harbour wall and quay that was built to create a harbour around the canal entrance) during the attack, the viaduct which connected the Mole to the mainland was to be destroyed. An old submarine filled with explosives was to sail under the viaduct and be blown up. Crews from block ships and submarine would be rescued by fast motor boats and taken back to destroyers waiting outside the harbour.

The elderly British cruiser HMS Vindictive, with a raiding party of 200 naval ratings and Royal Marines, was to land inside the Mole and destroy the heavy guns guarding it.

On that fateful evening of 22nd April 1918 a fleet of 76 vessels carrying 1700 men crossed the Channel. HMS Vindictive led the way commanded by Capt. Alfred Carpenter. HMS Vindictive was towing the passenger ferries Iris and Daffodil, commandeered from the River Mersey to carry the Royal Marines contingent for the assault on the Mole.

The operation began badly. The prepared smokescreen intended to cover the Vindictive as it landed its troops, proved ineffective in the face of unexpected winds. Under crippling fire the old cruiser moored in the wrong location, its guns effectively out of action. The angle of the ship's ramps was much steeper than had been expected and the troops were met by a hail of fire from the guns on the Mole and from German ships in the harbour. Because she had overshot her position, the troops had to fight through barbed wire defences whereas they had hoped to attack from the rear. However, the old submarine containing the explosives did destroy the Mole connecting the bridge to the shore after it exploded underneath it.

The loss of HMS Vindictive's guns was significant as without their crucial support the shore batteries remained untaken. It prevented the three ancient cruisers which were packed with concrete and now moved into the inner harbour, from halting and scuttling themselves in their correct locations at the narrow entrance to the canal.

Clearly things went disastrously wrong. HMS Vindictive returned home to Dover severely battered and bullet ridden but her crew were none-the-less hailed as heroes. Many officers and men had been killed and injured. There were 500 recorded casualties, of which 200 were fatal and 8 Victoria Crosses awarded.

Winston Churchill said, 'The Raid on Zeebrugge may well rank as the finest feat of arms in the Great War and certainly as an episode unsurpassed in the history of the

HMS Vindictive with battle damage

Royal Navy.' Though this was purely British propaganda on our part, in reality it did not hinder German operations from either port for more than just a few days.

Hundreds were injured and like Joseph would need to be hospitalised. Joseph required treatment for the shrapnel wound on his left upper arm, left side of his back, together with injuries to his 2nd and 3rd fingers on his right hand. He would have been sent, like many others, for a period of convalescence – and they would have been transported out by trains, ambulances and buses to various establishments up and down the country.

Armistice was declared at 11am on 11th November 1918. Joseph was not discharged and invalided out until 29th November 1918 – so he must have been quite badly injured.

NB A few months later HMS Vindictive was deployed in a similar operation at Ostend – the block ships again did not sink in their planned positions. This time Vindictive did not return, and was scuttled in Ostend harbour.

Foot note

A memorial statue was erected on 24th October, 2015 on Tower Bridge Road, Bermondsey, south London to Able Seaman Albert McKenzie. He was awarded the Victoria Cross for his brave actions on the Zeebrugge raid. He had been nominated by his shipmates. He sadly died in the Spanish flu epidemic a few months later in 1918.

The statue has the outline of a seaman in black metal and sits on top of a concrete plinth made from a section of the Zeebrugge harbour wall donated by the people of Flanders.

A portion of HMS Vindictive's bow section and anchor is now on display at Ostend harbour.

Mr Walter & Mrs Lily Hardman and Edith Hardman (Joseph's wife), 1960s

Wedding photo, May 22nd 1920.

Chapter Three

Kendal, Marriage and Photography

Joseph returned to Kendal where his mother was living at No 3 Park Avenue. He would no doubt be well looked after and when he was ready and able he would return to window cleaning and his enthusiasm to learn the art of photography.

Joseph married Edith Shaw, the girl he had known from childhood who had lived just across the road from him in Radcliffe. They tied the knot on 22nd May 1920 at the United Methodist Church in Radcliffe.

Over the years nothing much has been written or known about Joseph Hardman and so I was particularly grateful when I came across a lengthy article in the Penrith Herald, dated December 1951 (now the Cumberland and Westmorland Herald). The interview had been carried out by Tom Sarginson (who used the pseudonym 'Silver Pen') the editor, no less, who was the only person I have found who ever interviewed Joseph Hardman at length. These first six paragraphs are the lead into his lengthy, but informative, interview:

> *'There is probably no name in the 'Herald' more familiar to its readers than that of Mr Hardman. Week by week, year after year, that name has appeared in this newspaper – as indeed it does this week – almost invariably on the front page, sometimes inside as well, yet always in the same small type and always in the same laconic way*

Photo: Hardman

For twenty years Mr Joseph Hardman has taken photographs for the 'Herald' — pictures of the spring daffodils on Ullswater-side, summer sunshine in the Eden Valley, autumn foliage in Borrowdale, winter snow on Shap Fells — pictures, in fact, of the Lake country and its borderland in every aspect of scene and season, with the human element at work and at play as an integral part of the landscape.

Not only have his photographs become one of the most popular features of this paper, as numerous appreciative letters from our readers show, but they have achieved still greater prominence in countless national newspapers and periodicals, books and calendars. With his camera he has mirrored the life of Lakeland, its places and its people, in the minds of thousands who have never seen it — and thousands more who have.

His secret as a photographer is that he has the eye of an artist — an instinctive perception of what will make a good picture — coupled with the knowledge of just how and when to take it, the skill born of long experience, and, above all, the boundless enthusiasm of one whose work is his all-absorbing interest.

Yet, although he is widely known throughout the North — and particularly among the hills and dales of these two counties, where the sports and shows of the summer season would hardly be the same without his burly figure and cheery smile — there must be many of our readers whose acquaintance with Mr Hardman is limited to their admiration of his pictures.

Here, then, is something about the man who takes them, gleaned by a 'Herald' reporter in an interview at his home in Park Avenue, Kendal — an interview, incidentally, which was not without its difficulties, because Mr Hardman is far happier talking about his art and its subjects than about himself!'

We take up the rest of Tom Sarginson's article from the part played by Mr Clarence Webb.

From pastime to Profession

'The late Mr Clarence Webb, then head of the Kendal firm of florists and nurserymen,

Joseph with his window cleaning cart (Cambria Archive Centre, Kendal)

Mr Clarence Webb
(courtesy of Hilary Stoker)

in Burneside Road, several times mayor, was a member of the Photographic Society. It was Mr Webb's experienced guidance and infectious enthusiasm which inspired in the young amateur photographer the interest which was to result in the pastime of his leisure hours becoming his life's vocation.

For a time, he continued in other work (window cleaning) but was out and about with his camera whenever the opportunity presented itself; he sold a few pictures to newspapers, met with encouraging success and eventually decided to concentrate on photography as a means of earning his livelihood.'

It is not known definitely which camera he used to begin with, though one article mentioned a box camera and tripod, before moving on to the well-known large reflex plate camera and tripod.

'It was a happy decision, not only for himself but for the public at large, because the immense amount of personal enjoyment he has derived from his everyday doings as a roving cameraman has been shared by innumerable people to whom he has brought the beauty of Lakeland in pictorial form.

Mr Hardman is not a commercial photographer in the ordinary sense of the term. He had never, for instance, gone in for portraiture, wedding groups and the like.

He did none the less take certain portraits but of his choice – they had to have that extra something, character and individuality that kindled the spark of his interest – a veteran Dales man or a comely country lass – are among his best work.'

I discovered quite a few wedding photographs in Archives whereby the groom was in military uniform. Joseph clearly made the exception during the War.

One of his best known photographs was the Westmorland shepherd - Isaac Cookson

Isaac Cookson, Westmoreland shepherd (Museum of Lakeland Life and Industry, Lakeland Arts Trust)

Wintry conditions on Shap summit in the 1950s

– with a sheep on his shoulders and crook in hand – taken in 1952 at Mardale Shepherds Meet.

'Nor yet is he a Press photographer to whom the measure of a picture is its news value. Perhaps he is best described as 'an artist with a camera!' Strongest of all is the appeal of a fine landscape in his beloved Lake District.'

Joseph goes on to say, *"I have always found it difficult to regard photography as a business proposition. I make my business my pleasure and like to take just what I want – a subject that appeals to me."*

'Strongest of all is the appeal of a fine landscape in his beloved Lake District.'

"With a landscape, you can do what you like and it cannot talk back, but if you take a portrait you have to suit the sitter!"

Portraits with a Difference

The reporter goes on to say that Joseph *'Had also the news sense that is indispensable to the photographers who works for the time-conscious press. He has an uncanny knack of striking a topical note in his pictures, but it is still the artist in him that is uppermost. The scenic has a stronger pull than the sensational, and every photograph must be a picture in its own right. Whether it shows stranded lorries on a snowbound road or a railway train perilously perched on the edge of a viaduct, you may be sure it will nevertheless qualify as a first class landscape.*

He travels far and wide in pursuit of his pictures on special assignments for the newspapers and magazines with which he has freelance connections. But for the most part his travels are within the bounds of Cumberland and Westmorland or the adjacent areas of Lancashire and Yorkshire and even with that limitation they average something like 150-200 miles a week – always by taxi or in a friend's car, for he does not drive himself.'

To the Four Corners of Lakeland

'There is scarcely a corner of the Lake District or its immediate environs which he has not visited at one time or another – perhaps for a specific event or commission, perhaps just on chance, but always with something in his camera to show for it.
It is by no means uncommon for him to use three or four dozen plates when out for

Gale in Lake District, Ullswater. All that can be seen of the 98-foot pleasure steamer, Lady of the Lake, that sunk in the weekend gale. Nothing can be done until level goes down. 19/9/50

*the day, and how they mount up through the years! At that time (1950) he had accumulated 40-50,000 negatives of Lakeland alone, and the task of keeping even an approximate index can only be imagined. (*Edith*)*

His field work, three or four days a week, is the very breath of life to one who delights in going places, seeing things, meeting people, just as the spirit moves him – one who makes his work his holiday, in fact.'

The reporter waxes lyrical – *'He takes the weather just as it comes, for there is always something that will make a picture – frost or floods, sunshine or showers. Whatever the season, there are 'hardy annuals' to be covered – sports and shows in the summer, shepherd's meets in the autumn; skating and skiing in the winter, lambing-time in the spring, not to mention a thousand and one chance shots that catch the eye which is on the look-out for them. One of the reasons why he hired a taxi-driver or friend so he could sit quietly in the front passenger seat and with an eye could capture that unique shot he was always on the look-out for.'*

Shepherds Meets are where shepherds meet up to collect their strays identifying individuals by an ear or pop mark in the autumn. They usually end with a pie and pea supper and sing song 'Mardale' being one example.

'On these excursions, his wife Edith almost invariably accompanies him – "I would scarcely ever see him if I didn't," comments Mrs Hardman! – and she is a most valuable assistant in the practical business of the outing, whether it is in rounding up a flock of errant sheep on the fell side or posing unobtrusively beside a stream to add the finishing touch to the composition of a picture.'

Tom Sarginson goes on to mention – *'During the war years he also had the company of evacuee children from Tyneside, with whom he used to fill the car wherever he went and recalls many happy times with his adopted family. So do they evidently as some of them now grown-up and married call to see him when in the vicinity.'*

Off the Beaten Track

'Photographic expeditions up-hill and down dale in this part of the country inevitably involves frequent departure from the beaten track, and, as his pictures show, Mr

As they did it 100 years ago. Returning from Troutbeck Shepherds' Meet, to Round Hill Farm, Ambleside, with his strays and a lame one on horseback.

Hardman not only gets to some out-of-the-way places but also contrives to reach some well-nigh inaccessible positions in order to get just the right angle on his subject. To those who are familiar with his Falstaffian figure it is a miracle how he ever manages it.

Remarkably agile for all his ample proportions, he can put to shame many a lesser man, notwithstanding the encumbrance of a weighty camera. He makes no secret of the fact that he tips the scales at sixteen stones and was at one time three stones more.

Joseph confesses that he keeps the walking to a minimum whereby the reporter adds, 'I am very fond of the fells, but I like best to see them from my bay window!'

Dull Days in the Darkroom

'To Mr Hardman, there is just one drawback about this care-free life out-of-doors existence. Sooner or later his peregrinations must come to an end and he must return home to the Stygian solitude of his dark room to fulfil the irksome task of producing the prints.'

Joseph said, "I enjoy going out and getting the pictures but I don't like the developing and printing. That is why I prefer taking photographs for the Press; once I turn the picture out, I am done with it."

'Nor has he much time for the textbook technicalities of his profession, preferring to rely on what he calls 'guesswork' but what is really the good judgement which comes automatically from years of experience – so much so that he does not even possess an exposure meter, the instrument photographers use for measuring light intensity. He is especially fond of working against the light – a tricky but effective aspect of photography in which he has exceptional skill.

He always uses plates, never films, and for the tools of his trade he has four or five big reflex cameras, which he considers to give the best results in the pictorial type of work in which he specialises.'

Camera in the Waterfall

And thereby hangs a tale – the tale of the camera that should have hung but didn't! As a result, it might provide a worth-while object for a treasure hunt for any adventurous

Skelwith Falls, Ambleside

soul who cares to try to probe the depths of the pool at the foot of Skelwith Falls, near Ambleside.

It happened about Christmas time one year during the war, when the fells were under snow, the falls were in flood, and Mr Hardman was engaged in his eternal quest for pictures. Walking down beside the falls, he had his camera case on the clasp, but with the straps unbuckled, when – as, of course, it would at such a moment the clasp sprang open and out dropped the camera, plumb into the stream and down to the bottom of the waterfall!

And there it still lies - £50 to £70 worth at present-day prices – for although Mr Hardman has tried to locate it in times of drought, his search has proved fruitless.

In case you are interested, Mr Hardman says that, while the camera will naturally be ruined, the lens – a particularly good one – should still be none the worse!

Twenty years of press photography

'So much, then, for the daily round of a man who sees life mostly through a view-finder. Now for something about the success he has achieved with the pictures for which, and by which, he lives.'

Tom Sarginson goes on to mention that *'The 'Herald' was one of the first papers which accepted Mr Hardman's work when he ventured into Press photography around 1930, and it has used his pictures almost every week ever since. But in the intervening period he has established a reputation far beyond the readership of this newspaper.*

For some years his photographs have appeared regularly in such papers as 'The Times', 'Manchester Guardian' and 'Yorkshire Post', not to mention what used to be called 'Penny Dailies'. But perhaps the greatest demand for them has developed in the highly selective field of the 'glossy' magazines such as 'Sport and Country' and 'The Illustrated London News' and those with a specifically outdoor flavour like 'Country Life' and 'The Field' often for use on the cover.

Foot note -
Penny Dailies - cheap tabloid style newspapers – half broadsheets.

In this year's (1951) Christmas Annual, among a very fine collection of photographs, his 'Autumn scene at Haweswater' has the distinction of being the only one to which a whole page is devoted.'

Combined operations in the Isle of Man

'For 'Sport and Country' he has undertaken a number of special commissions, frequently working in conjunction with Mr Sydney Moorhouse, of Bolton-le-Sands, a well-known journalist and broadcaster on country topics. A recent occasion of that kind was at this year's Royal Manx Agricultural Show (1951), which they covered jointly, then staying on in the Isle of Man for a few days to carry out a commission for Ferguson Tractors on the farm of Mr G. E. Christian, near Douglas, who had won the prize for the best stocked farm in the island. Mr Christian, incidentally, specialises in Shorthorns and flies to England to make purchases at Penrith sales.

They also paid a visit to Derbyshire to obtain material for an illustrated article on the farm of Mr Ashton Priestley, winner of the championship at this year's International Sheep Dog Trials (for which Mr Hardman is the official photographer), and attended the National Ploughing Championships at Tadcaster.

Then there are annual engagements at Southport Flower Show, the Royal Lancashire Agricultural Show, and other leading events of the kind all over the North, quite apart from a full program of Lakeland fixtures during the summer season.'

Pictures for books and brochures

'Mr Hardman has also contributed several series of pictures for feature articles in 'Picture Post' and does a good deal for farming journals, while examples of his work supplied through agencies appear in a wide range of periodicals.

Mr Hardman has provided photographic illustrations for numerous books, among them Mr Moorhouse's 'The British Sheep Dog' and several by Mr W. T. Palmer, and he is constantly being called upon by the publishers of pictorial turn-over calendars, guide books, advertising brochures etc. In the latter category he has done a considerable amount for the Blackpool Tower Circus and for Morecambe Corporation.

He receives many requests for prints of his photographs which have appeared in the

Press or elsewhere. Only recently, a 'Manchester Guardian' reader wrote asking for one which was published in that newspaper in 1939!

In view of all these commitments, it is hardly surprising that, despite the persuasive efforts of many admirers of his pictures, Mr Hardman has not gone in for exhibiting other than locally. 'I simply have not the time,' he says, 'It is as much as I can do to keep pace with Press requirements.'

This is a pity, nevertheless because his work is of a standard which would qualify it for display at any of the great national or international salons (galleries). A dozen products of his genius were an outstanding attraction at the Festival of Britain exhibition at Kendal this year (1951).'

But Mr Hardman is of that happy breed of men to whom the laurels of their calling are of less account than the abiding satisfaction of the daily round in a congenial task. He is a man who loves his work for its sake, and you can see it in every picture he takes!

'The Herald' was one of the first papers which accepted Mr Hardman's work when he ventured into Press photography around 1930, and it has used his pictures almost every week ever since. But in the intervening period he has established a reputation far beyond the readership of this newspaper.'

One of Joseph's special memories during the war was when he took photos of evacuees for the Ministry of Information. The taxi drivers who conveyed him and his wife around the countryside were apparently able to buy petrol at any garage without being rationed – much to the envy of their friends.

The Herald used to publish several editions – Keswick, Ambleside, Alston, Kirkby Stephen and Appleby – 2,000 copies of each.

Tom Sarginson, author of the above interview, sadly died in December 1951 - the month this article, which was a two page spread, was published. Tom was the writer of 'Notes and Comments' for 54 years. Beginning his working life with the Penrith Herald as a compositor, he gradually moved over to the journalistic side, his first 'Notes and Comments' appearing in 1896. He was acting editor in 1903 until 1913 when he officially became editor and was known under his pen name 'Silver Pen' throughout Cumberland and Westmorland until his death at 81.

Tom Sarginson

(Cumberland and Wstermoreland Herald)

Edith & Joseph

Chapter Four

Later Years

Joseph continued being a very successful freelance photographer, working not only for the Westmorland Gazette and Penrith Herald for many years and farming papers such as Farmers Weekly, but also for all the national papers and magazines. In particular the Daily Mail, News Chronicle, the Manchester Guardian, they liked his scenes of Lakeland. He took more than 60,000 glass plates (negatives) that we know of with his bulky reflex camera and in later years with more modern cameras.

In the Kendal Archives I have found albums full of family photographs taken at various times of the year, together with some of the many hundreds of black and white pictures clear and crisp as if they were taken only yesterday.

On turning over some of the photographs I was delighted to find that Joseph had written in biro on some of them. His captions are well written, well thought out, accurate, humorous – giving details of where they were taken, if it was an event, what it was, the winners or who they were and where, also the date and, of course, his copyright stamp. They always had suitable captions so that when the newspaper or magazine received them their work had been done. Plus if the picture was an 'Exclusive' it was importantly printed in capitals.

I can only surmise from this information that these would be copies of some of the ones he had sent off to the various newspapers and magazines for publication – they were certainly all excellent photographs. No doubt the information was that which Edith had recorded in her little black book, which were so important and he would always check that she had noted them all – *'Did you get that Edith?' 'Oh, stop worrying,'* she would reply. Sadly these little black books have not been saved.

Joseph had also marked on the back of some of his photographs, indicating the size, or trimming down to make smaller or if an imperfection appeared removing it.

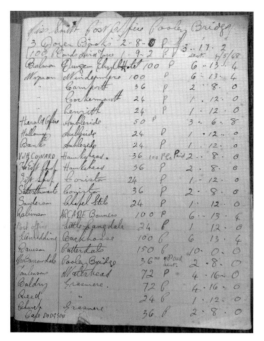

Sample of Joseph's paperwork, 1948

Some, I noted, had entry forms cut out from newspapers, eg 'Yorkshire Post' for entry into photographic competitions and the closing date for entry was glued to the back. Joseph had filled in his details in biro and presumably sent the relevant ones off.

It is interesting to note that in a package of some thirty-five glass plates held in a box in Kendal Archives, each slide was in an individual envelope and hand written on the front by Joseph - specifying what was on that particular plate and also giving a number.

He was said to have taken three or four dozen glass plates (photographs) each time he was out. He would have needed to have had a good index system to enable him to find a particular glass plate or photograph amongst so many – after all, it was his living as well as his life's vocation.

We know that some of the photographs he would be commissioned to take by a newspaper, magazine or Agency, would be paid with expenses for travelling to the location and taking the photographs. Some he would send to an Agency for them to sell on, others would be for his regular newspapers and magazines.

The pictures are amazing and each one tells a story. From the available photographs it is possible to see the vast variety and quality he had taken. They demonstrate the events he went to in the calendar year, the places he went to, and his obvious love of everyday rural life. The subjects are endless, displaying life in the places he went to all over Lakeland and beyond.

He particularly liked the farming year: the lambing, ploughing and sowing, thinning and gathering turnips, hay-time, cattle, sheep and lambs, sheep shearing, poultry, harvest, stooks, threshers and bracken harvesting. He attended shows, gatherings, sports, hunting, fairs eg at Brough and Appleby.

He loved the Lakes and took many photographs in and around them at different times of the year. People at work were another popular theme - blacksmiths, spinning, basket making, stacking peat, gathering damsons, cutting sea-washed turf, gathering apples, scare-crow competitions, hiring days at various towns.

The list and subjects is endless. His pictures usually involved people and animals, with always some form of movement – never just a scene. He has recorded the many changes in agriculture and machinery. He went back time and time again to the same locations at different times of the year.

Joseph's house was, needless to say filled with newspapers and magazines and these would have been sent to him by the newspapers and publications which had used his photographs.

It must be remembered that he would be out for full days at a time. Sometimes he took his models – other times it would just be Edith, and the taxi driver – but the planning and preparation were so important.

Joseph's choice of living in the Lake District provided him with excellent themes for his photography in which we can take delight. Joseph turned some of his photographs into postcards, and these he distributed into the many local Lake District Post Offices,

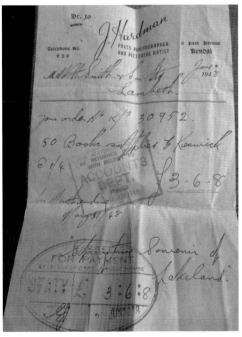

(Cumbria Archive Centre, Kendal)

W. H. Smiths, shops, Youth Hostels, Public Houses, hotels amongst others in towns and villages – and these would be bought and posted by the early tourists to their friends and relatives back home.

This surely shows how well he did and how he circulated his cards to the little outlets throughout the Lake District by post or taxi. One example of the quantities sold at this time is a letter from Mrs Smith at the Post Office, Pooley Bridge, Penrith dated 5/5/48 ordering 1000 postcards of the Pony Club at Pooley Bridge in black and white.

In 1948 Joseph produced a Springtime

Shoeing at Crosthwaite Smithy, Westmoreland (Museum of Lakeland Life and Industry, Lakeland Arts Trust)

Making swill baskets (Cumbria Archive Centre, Kendal)

Souvenir of Lakeland View book which did particularly well and these were also sold at W H Smith and Wyman & Sons bookstalls at railway stations throughout the Lake District area and into Lancashire. He was obviously in his heyday.

They would have led busy, full lives. Edith would have her own jobs to do – looking after the models – seeing that Joseph had everything – preparing picnics and importantly recording all the details of every picture that Joseph took.

Not only that but Joseph was, for a time, still working as a window cleaner (probably to augment the money coming into the house) and Edith had the house to keep and run. This was a business, so in the afternoons Joseph would return to Park Avenue and have to go upstairs into his dark room and develop the glass plates that he would be sending off to Manchester for the all-important following morning's paper, or further afield to magazines or weeklies. He would have a time constraint to catch the evening post at the Main Post Office in Stricklandgate, or to send them on the train to Manchester, where his brother-in-law Charles used to collect the envelope/parcel and 'hot foot' it round to the relevant newspaper for inclusion in the morning edition. He would also have his own mail to attend to and also the task of delivering his postcards to the Post Offices and shops around the Lake District for selling to the early tourists. The purchase of glass plates and Ilfords photographic paper would be bought locally.

He enjoyed holidays with Edith in Blackpool and visits to Morecambe. During these visits he incorporated a considerable amount of advertising and publicity work for both Blackpool Tower Circus and Morecambe Corporation.

Bill Mitchell, former reporter and editor of The Cumbria magazine for many years gives us a further insight into the way that Joseph took his photographs, how they used to receive a batch of whole-plate black and white glossy prints from Joseph almost weekly and they would regularly appear in their magazine from 1951. He goes on to say how Joseph used the light to his best advantage and taking shots which perhaps other photographers would not – taking the pictures against the light and was not discouraged when the shadows lengthened and the light began to fade. He would find that odd shaft of sunlight to bring up the subject against a dark background. Only once did he see him at work and this is what he writes:-

'His wife set up the heavy tripod just across the road from the church (St Martins) at Bowness. Carefully he attached to it a large plate camera. This would be no 'snapshot' but a carefully composed study. He waited until the lighting conditions were right. The photograph was exposed, the plate sheathed, removed and replaced with another. It was a languid, thoughtful operation.'

In recognition for all the years the Cumbria magazine had included his photographs in their monthly magazine, they published a 72 page paperback book containing his photographs in 1967 titled 'Lakeland Through the Year'. I was fortunate enough to buy one recently in a second hand bookshop in Hawes, together with a second edition copy of the 1964-65 Cumberland Official Guide with Map. Costing originally two shillings this was filled with local information, advertisements and many of Joseph's photographs of the area.

Joseph sold 3 Park Avenue to Mr Robert Bowman in 1967 but the couple continued to live on in the house. In later years Joseph suffered from diabetes and had to give up photography in 1969 due to ill health. A newspaper cutting from Cumbria Lake District Life in July 1970, with the caption 'Personalities Mr & Mrs Joseph Hardman' shows a photograph of Joseph and Edith sitting side by side on a bench on Blackpool promenade with the tower in the background: 'Celebrating their golden wedding which they did quietly with relations.'

In another newspaper cutting bearing the same photo it says 'That although Mr Hardman gave up photography more than 12 months ago, it continues to be his main interest, and boxes of prints fill the house.'

They would live out their remaining years quietly together, a devoted couple – remembering all the places they had been, the many people they had come across and photographed.

Joseph, sadly, died a year later on 21st September 1972, aged 79 years. An item appeared in the Lancashire Evening Post with just a few lines, 'Joseph Hardman died in hospital. Funeral Parkside Cemetery. He leaves a wife.'

Charles, Edith's brother saw to the estate and nearly five thousand glass plates, together with camera and equipment were donated to Abbot Hall (Museum of

Lakeland Life and Industry), Kendal. Edith donated a large number of photographs to both the Carnegie Library and the Archives Department at County Hall, Kendal and gifted to their two nephews, Eric and Kenneth.

Edith never really got over Joseph's death and in later years went into Maudes Meadow old peoples' home in Kendal. She, sadly, died on 2nd June 1978, in her 80s. Both now lie at peace together in an unmarked grave in Parkside Cemetery, only a short distance from where they lived.

Golden wedding

Family photo from Eric Shaw

l to r: Eric, Charles (father), Edith (aunt), Mary (mother), Annie (aunt)

Chapter Five

The People who Remember Joseph and Edith

I have been fortunate to meet some of the people whom Joseph knew, either from the farms he visited or some of the young people and evacuees who acted as models in his photographs to help enhance a scene and bring it to life. It is from these youngsters (now adults) that we are able to glean more of an insight into Joseph and Edith's life of photography - especially during the late 1930-1950s.

Eric Shaw – nephew – Lancaster – 11th February 2013

Eric's father, Charles, was Edith's brother and they used to live nearby in Lowton Street, Radcliffe.

He does not remember seeing much of them, but remembers the family getting post cards sent to them – taken by Joseph with a message on the back from his Aunt Edith. *'They were usually about family news, commenting about the weather or family visits. The writing was all over – every little space taken up – up the sides as well as where the text was meant to be put.'* These are proudly kept in a well-thumbed album – the writing is clearly visible through the plastic and easily read.

3 Park Avenue
Kendal

Dear Cissy – Charlie
We have just come back, Monday from another lovely run to Thirlmere and seen the big Christmas tree cut down for Albert Square, Manchester – my word what a job, about ten men and a horse it has taken all day. How do you like this picture taken last Saturday. The Hunts man bringing the Hounds to Mardale Hunt. Saturday we went to Keswick. Love from all at Kendal.

Christmas tree for Manchester from Thirlmere (Cumbria Archive Centre, Kendal)

A load of Christmas trees and girls at Thirlmere

Eric told me, *'I remember visiting my aunt and uncle in Kendal and how the house was filled with boxes of photographs, glass plates, yellow Ilford boxes containing photographic paper, newspapers and magazines piled high everywhere - in the rooms, along the hall and up the stairs.'* He smiled and then said, *'Once Aunt Edith was making the tea in the kitchen and had put down the bottle of milk and couldn't find it!*

He showed me a photograph and said, *'Uncle Joseph took this picture of me sitting on a rock overlooking Grasmere.'* He did not visit often but he remembers meeting his uncle at Riggs bakery and cafe at the top of Lowther Street, Kendal for tea.

'My Dad, Charles, used to collect the photographs off the train in Manchester for Uncle Joseph and it was Dad's task to get them to the various Dailies on time so that they could be in the following morning's papers such as the Daily Herald, Manchester Guardian, Daily Mail and News Chronicle.'

It was important that it got into a particular daily first before any other photographer – 'a scoop.' This was doubly important as he was a freelance photographer and was either asked to do it as an 'assignment' paid for beforehand or just that it was a topical picture – therefore an enhanced rate was paid.

Michael Bottomley – Architect and artist – 15th February 2013

I was fortunate to meet up with Michael Bottomley, a retired architect and artist, who lived on the outskirts of Windermere. He remembers Joseph from the 1950s, and used to work for Donald Haigh at their architects' office at the bottom of Lowther Street, Kendal.

'I used to go up the road for my lunch to Riggs Café, which was at the corner of Lowther Street with Highgate on the left. The bakery was on the ground floor and upstairs was the café where you went for lunch (this was in the days before take-away food). It was not big upstairs, about ten tables, about three feet by two foot six square with tablecloths, chairs and waitress service. Two windows looked onto Highgate and one onto Lowther Street with a small yard behind. The back of the tearoom on the right was taken up by the kitchen and the stairs up from the bakery. It was after the war so food was still in short supply but meals were nice but plain. I used to go up there from time to time and Mr Hardman would come up for his lunch as well – not

daily as he would be out taking photographs and other regulars would be there as well, Mr Pickthall he worked at Martins Bank, now Barclays and Mr Richards and his wife had a chemists shop near the Parish Church. There would sometimes be a queue up the stairs of people waiting to get seated for lunch and we would push past in order to get seated. If anyone enquired why we were doing this we would say, 'We are regular customers!' So obviously we got talking from time to time.'

Michael also said, *'Joseph was a nice chap, well-built, would be about my height about six feet. I remember him saying that he had to take photographs to Lancaster to get the post or to make sure they got on the train as the post had already been collected in Kendal. His wife, Edith, came occasionally. He was really an artist, a bit ahead of his time re models – movement in the pictures – you could always tell a Hardman picture, they had that extra something – stood out from the rest – sometimes hard to differentiate from Ken Shepherd.'* (another Kendal photographer who worked previously for Westmorland Gazette before setting up on his own in 1935. He was a friend of Alfred Wainwright and later had two books published – when in his 70's.)

Michael, sadly died in January 2015

MARY WHITWELL – 24th June 2014

I met Mary, a retired farmer's wife, at her bungalow, looking down over Windermere on a sunny afternoon in late June 2014.

The views were terrific. You could see for miles around with Windermere in the foreground together with the many Lakeland Fells nestling against one another with the Langsdales to the right. It was simply beautiful and I can see why this was a favourite location for Joseph to come and how he became friends with the family.

She proudly told me, *'Joseph and his wife visited many times and became good friends. He loved the spring and used to take lots of photographs of this little paddock at the farm because it was full of rocks and daffodils in spring and a wonderful backdrop of the fells. The daffodils now have been well nibbled by horses so have not been prevalent for some time.'*

John Whitwell, Low Longmire, Windermere

Rescued from the drift

Joseph came mainly in lambing time. Sometimes he would bring a couple of girls he used as models. I lived in a neighbouring farm and I married John in 1950 and because John had modelled such a lot for Mr Hardman he asked if he would take our wedding photographs and he agreed.' She proudly showed me and said, '*A large photograph of our wedding had been hanging up in Brockhole Visitors Centre together with a similar sized one with sheep he had taken. When they were updating the premises we managed to obtain the one with our wedding but unfortunately the one with the sheep had already gone elsewhere.'*

She remembered them well, '*Mrs Hardman was a very nice lady. They took many photos – a particular one taken of John rescuing some sheep by digging them out of deep snowdrifts. We got a surprise one day when a relation in Canada told us about looking in one of their local shoe shop windows and seeing a large metal 'K Shoe' advertisement displayed picturing John and some sheep. They were amazed and thought it was wonderful!*

Tommy (retired blacksmith and volunteer fireman) and Mary Bland, his wife – 27th June 2013

I visited them at their home in June 2013 and Tommy said, '*I can remember him in Kentmere in 1941-2 – 'Every year at sheep shearing (clipping) time we did particular farms at set dates helping one another out. Joseph Hardman would come and always wore a big jacket with huge pockets to store glass plates in. Rooke Howe was the first Monday July; Kentmere Hall was first Tuesday in July and Hartrigg first Wednesday, Twenty people were shearing, plus another catching, marking, and all the other jobs to be done like wrapping wool and such like. After milking, was the clipping, then we went home to milk and came back for three or four hours to play nap. Whilst clipping there would be barrels of beer. We clipped several hundred in a day – we used creels to put the sheep on to clip, some did this without and just clipped down on the ground.*

Joseph went up the ladder backwards – to find a good location to get a good picture of us all shearing – he would sit down with camera and take them. He used his jacket pockets to store his glass plates. He was just a nice jovial man that everyone accepted.'

Clipping day at Brockstone (Cumbria Archive Centre, Kendal)

Clara Black (Cumbria Archive Centre, Kendal)

'Before I was married (lived at Park House, Staveley Head) I was in the Young Farmers and Joseph Hardman always took a lot of photographs for them, stock judging and local shows. When I married I moved to Bridgestone and we all helped one another at the different farms. We collected the sheep from the east side – the sheep were hefted – so the farmers would go up the fell and gather them altogether and bring down all the sheep for Brockstone, High Bridge and Bridgestone.

If we thought it was going to be a hot day they would go and bring down the sheep earlier maybe 4.30am – if too hot bad for sheep, dogs and clippers.

In those days we would have farm workers and sometimes they lived in farm cottages and in wartime we sometimes had prisoners (lived in) mostly Italians. Germans sometimes came out in a wagon from the (Bela) camp at Milnthorpe – but that was before I was married.

We all had our jobs to do. Women mostly wrapped the fleeces -
Rolled them inside out. Later when they were packed into large sacks the children would help to pack them. We clippers used creels – the number of clippers varied. We had 300 Rough Fell and usually had eight or ten clippers. 8 or 8.30am coffee and scones about 11am. Then sandwiches 12.30 and plenty to drink – barrel of beer – lemonade for a shandy. Usually finished about 6.30pm. Then a meal in the house – meat and sandwiches.

Young Farmers Club at Park House, Staveley Head, in May 1945.

Joseph Hardman used to just appear, mostly by himself. When his wife came she usually stayed in the background.

Interview with Andrew Cannon (son of Bill Cannon one of Joseph's taxi drivers) at his home in Kendal – September 2014

'My father, William Cannon, lived at 5 Collin Road and after coming back from the war he worked for Billy Beetham's taxi business (Fleece Inn Yard) *and when he retired in the 1950s he took over. Billy used to live in Burneside Road just opposite the turn-off into the Police Station. Before the war my father had been a milkman – the first to have his name printed on the bottle and when he was called up he only had a fortnight to sell the business.*

He had a black Austin FX1 London Pattern Taxi and bought extra taxis as business increased. Mr Hardman would ring up, mostly at night, saying it was going to be a good day tomorrow I want to be out. He was after photos of such and such a place – mostly agricultural. So my Dad would have to find a driver to do his work whilst he took Mr Hardman out for the day. Since my Dad lived in Collin Road it was just a short distance down to Park Avenue to pick him up and load up all his camera equipment and go out for the day.

I can remember his wife she was a nice lady and they got on quite well and occasionally she would ask my Dad if he would like to bring his family along as well. My Dad had a big 6-seater - Austin Sixteen – originally owned by the Ministry of Food - and we used to all go out for the day. I would be about three or four years old when he took a photograph of me amongst the daffodils feeding lambs with a bottle of milk at a farm at Yealand Conyers.

Dad would come in at night at 7pm tired after a long day and would be having his tea when the phone would ring and it would be Mr Hardman saying, 'We are going out tomorrow, Bill!' That was how it worked.

Dad used to get prints from Joseph and he would present him with a calendar. He had also saved paper cuttings out of the paper of some of the scenes they had taken and sometimes the taxi was pictured.

In those days Dad used to drive a lot of business people around as there were few cars and sometimes would take them out for an afternoon run (drive*).'*

Andrew remembered clearing Joseph's house out with his Dad at Mrs Hardman's request and they took a lot of glass plates to Abbot Hall. *'They were 4" x 3"s and each of them would be in paper and then in a magazine box for safe keeping.'*

Bill Cannon in a boat at Derwentwater

Taxi going through the ford at Winster

Chapter Six

The Models

It is impossible to go any further before mentioning the important part played by Joseph's models whom he took out with him in the taxi accompanied by Edith, who sat with them in the back. These were schoolgirls whom he asked to accompany him on weekend journeys into the Lake District and would ask them to dress in suitable clothing according to the time of year and country way of life. Then when he came to a suitable location, whether it was by a lake, fell or farm, he would ask the girls to walk, stand or simply take in the view.

In the meantime, Joseph would have carried his heavy reflex camera and glass plates out of the car and set it up on the large tripod that he or the taxi driver had already positioned. When he was pleased conditions were just right – he would take the photograph. Edith had an important part to play – that of noting down all the details in her little black book, the time, date, location and of course who was in the photograph and mark the slide accordingly.

He always wanted his photographs to have people in the foreground not just a beautiful view – they had to have movement - 'every picture tells a story'. The vital information which Edith noted down was required later when he developed the pictures to send off to the many newspapers or magazines, or simply to store and maybe use at a later date. Sometimes, the figure in the photograph would be Edith or she would be with the girls. At other times it would be a farmer ploughing a field, a shepherd tending his flock or a farmer's wife or child feeding ducks or hens in a farmyard. He knew what scenes he wanted and how best to photograph them – this was the artist in him. When he had captured it you could see he was happy.

Two evacuees from Liverpool enjoying life on a Lakeland Farm

Mary Cowperthwaite (nee Nevinson), Bannisdale Head, Selside

I visited Sylvia Deacon (nee Jenkins) at her home in Windermere – 19th February 2013

Sylvia is a petite well-dressed lady who had worked at the Windermere Steamboat Museum which, sadly, closed and was demolished in 2014. This is to make way

for the new purpose built museum, - 'Windermere Jetty' funded by nearly seventeen million pounds from the Heritage Lottery Fund. She fondly remembers Joseph and Edith and how she had indeed become like part of their family.

She told me of how St. John's School from South Shields had been evacuated to Kendal at the beginning of the war and how they had used the hall in the Salvation Army buildings. This was on the left as you went down Blackhall Yard and eventually brought you out onto Stramongate at St George's Theatre. This is no longer here and was knocked down to make way for the Telephone Exchange and car parking on Blackhall Road in 1966.

Sylvia with a basket of flowers

She proudly brought out her two albums full of black and white photographs that Joseph had taken and said, *'When he took photographs he usually gave a copy to the persons in the pictures so they had one to keep and stamped on back of each in black ink - 'Joseph Hardman, Kendal. Copyright'.*

Sylvia told me proudly how she first met Joseph. *'I had been walking with my friend, Joan McCartney, in Kirkland and Mr Hardman was on his bicycle and stopped to speak to us. I knew Joan was already one of his models. She was a very good one because she could be photographed from any angle - dark curly hair and plump face. He asked me if I would like to accompany Joan when she went out with his wife and him on his photographic trips – to which I readily agreed and that was the beginning of my twenty years close friendship with the Hardman family.'*

'I was living at the time with the Pickles family in Aynam Road, they were my hosts - Mr Pickle's was a wool merchant, his wife worked in ammunitions, near Ambleside, and their son was in the Air Force.'

'I would be about fifteen or sixteen at the time and learning shorthand, typing and bookkeeping at the Commercial School at the Allen Technical Institute. Miss Corbet, a secretary at Martins Bank taught us shorthand in the evening. We had Miss Blunt and Mr Morland as our teachers at school and there were over ten of us. I remember the teachers did not like Mr Hardman just taking us direct from school and just occasionally it was not approved of.'

'In the early days when I was sixteen and working I remember Mr Hardman cleaning shop windows,– he always used his bicycle and Walter, his brother, was a bit bow legged. Mrs Walter Hardman was a refined lady and they lived at Murley Moss and then eventually moved to Lytham. We used to go for meals at Christmas and I remember sledging down the hill in the garden at Murley Moss, it was lovely. They had no children of their own. We had some lovely times and of course Joseph took photographs which I still have of us all.'

'Other models I remember were the McDonald triplets who stayed at the opticians in Kirkland; Joan McCartney stayed at the Hayton's on Glebe Road with their daughter, who was another model. Mrs Marion Jennings (maiden name Humphreys) she was originally from Mealbank - 'wifie' as she was called and used to advertise accommodation in the paper.'

'Mr Hardman didn't drive or have a car and he used Beetham's Taxi's. I think the driver was the owner Mr Beetham and he lived on Burneside Road and charged so much per mile. He had one or two drivers but usually it was Mr Beetham himself

with his daughter who was a similar age to me. I remember a Mr Tatham drove us once (he used to live at Clyde Cottage, down the side of the Sawyers Arms, Stricklandgate – under the narrow archway and his old Austin Cambridge car just managed to squeeze through).'

She fondly remembers going to Sports Days and other beautiful days out in the Lakes. *'Mr Hardman always sat in the front and Mrs Hardman and us girls in the back and if Mr Hardman saw anything that caught his eye, he stopped the taxi, whether it be a huntsman with hounds, or a particular Lakeland view eg Wastwater, Elterwater, Ennerdale. One of our favourite places was Swindale Farm, near Shap. Very often Mrs Hardman would make picnic teas – we would have a big picnic basket, with table cloth to lay on the grass. There would be plenty to eat and a flask of tea. I remember we used to sing sometimes in the way back, 'If you were the only girl in the world.'*

'Looking back there always seemed to be a lot of sunny days when we were out taking photographs. Mr Hardman was a generous man and we went to the best cafés and hotels for meals, he spent his money. He did like you to be in pretty dresses, I remember he was not pleased when I bought a grey one. The incident when Mr Hardman dropped his camera at the waterfall – I remember well, I was there that day and I was lowered down on a rope to try and locate the ill-fated camera but couldn't find it.'

'Often we went out at short notice – there would be about twenty models – but over the course of time. They were always very nice to us and Mrs Hardman was very motherly.'

'I remember going to the Kendal Museum to see an exhibition of his photographs.' (Festival of Britain 1951)

'I married when I was 35 but still kept in touch with the Hardmans'

Delia Shaw (nee Bowman) at her home in Kendal – 20th July 2013

Delia's family had moved to the Kendal area in 1941 to escape the bombing in Liverpool during the Second World War. She told me about how she met Joseph Hardman and became a model.

Joe Weir, the huntsman bringing the hounds to Mardale Hunt

'I would be about sixteen when one of my friends from the High School in Kendal, asked me if I would like to join her to spend a day in the Lakes with the photographer, Joseph Hardman. Older friends from school had done this and I thought perhaps now they wanted a change and to do other things at weekends. So I said, 'Yes, I would.'

He would decide if it was a good day and would telephone early on a Saturday morning. I don't know whether he picked me up or I rode to Park Avenue on my bike, I can't remember. He would maybe ask if I could bring a friend. It would be either Mary Wadeson from Oxenholme or Margaret Porch, two of my High School friends. There was also Ann Legget, who was a year older than me, and a chemist's daughter from Bowness. It was quite open you didn't ask permission. You would never think a thing about it then. It would sound suspicious nowadays having a gaggle of girls going out as we did.

'Right, we will go off,' he would say. We would wear suitable country clothing and would be on our way by 9.30am. He would have an idea where he was going and there we would go and it was Beetham's taxis, always the same driver.

Off we would go and Mr Hardman would sit in the front and we would get up into the Lakes. He would tell the driver to stop if he had seen something and, of course, Mrs

Hardman was with us sitting in the back. She would help him out with the tripod - this was quite a paraphernalia to set it up (and his heavy bulky reflex camera) *but it was what they did in those days. She was in charge of the* (glass) *plates and had the note book, kept the numbers and the records. He would choose the site.*

Maybe she and I would be chosen to do something in the foreground or break the foreground. It was wonderful it was always a lovely day because he didn't choose wet days. We would drive into the Lakes and he would always stop for lunch and he had his favourite cafes/restaurants, one was on the left going down into Bowness (Huttons, Crag Brow) *on the first floor and we would perhaps have lunch there. He had a very good appetite.*

Then we used to go to Hawkshead and there was a lady who made the most amazing pastries and cakes and so on and served teas and it was in Hawkshead Hall. You entered by going up stone steps – the Institute. You went into this first floor room and oh, he loved those pastries! We went mainly at weekends, not often in the summer holidays.

He did not speak much, his mind was on the scenery, on the light and what he could find. He must have told the driver where he wanted to go but I never heard that part of the conversation. He was quietly spoken.

Margaret and I remember one day we went up to Keswick and we went to an outcrop of rocks, it was lambing time and there was a shepherd there with his dog and that was lovely. He knew it like the back of his hand really.'

Did the models always get photographs afterwards?

'Probably he did go back afterwards and give them a photo, certainly that is how I got my photographs when I was there. I don't remember going into the western side of the Lake District very much. We did not go up to farms as much, often just seeing them working as we were driving along and took advantage of the opportunity. He wasn't taking the photos of farmers as much as opportunities with us to create a picture, I suppose. He seemed to be on good terms with all the farmers where we stayed or stopped. I remember about seagulls, if they were there on the lakeside Mrs Hardman would be feeding them – we always had masses of birds round us. I think she always must have had a bag of bread in the car.

We would go out about every other weekend (for 2 or 3 years) *during that period judging by the number of photographs I've got. Back home about 5 o'clock then he had the job of developing all the plates he had taken that day. He would take them upstairs to his dark room. Then they would have been sent by post to the newspapers and magazines of the day and even to America. All the girls married and went away. I was usually on my own and Mrs Hardman went to look after Joseph.*

We used to drive along and you became quite lethargic and I suddenly thought I should be walking in the fells, I shouldn't just be sitting in the back of the taxi and that's because maturity comes on and you have other things to do.

My father (Mr R A Bowman) *was in insurance and then the war came and he decided to retire, he inherited some small properties in Sunderland and Liverpool from his mother and so he retired very early.*

'He had time and offered to drive for Mr Hardman because it was father's pleasure to see the Lakes and was more than happy to watch Mr Hardman at work and it was lovely for someone to have retired and have this interest. The war interrupted so much. I think he enjoyed Mr Hardman's knowledge of the Lake District – witnessing the way he worked. Mr Hardman was eight years older than Dad.

Delia, Mr & Mrs Shaw, and Edith, Xmas 1950

I didn't go at that time because I had found more things to do as in getting engaged and finding somewhere to live, marrying and then having children, of course.

I remember his photographs being in both National and International press. His photographs of damson time up the Lyth valley and blossom those are the sort of photographs I liked best, rather than social, domestic activities where the farmers would be – that to me is the historical record that he made. He was quiet and gentle.

Interesting to see how he worked and the equipment he used. How many people can use a camera of that age today? Those little books were very important. I remember Joseph always checked Edith had noted everything down and Edith saying, 'Oh, stop worrying!' I always remember that.'

She proudly showed me a collage her family had put together for her 80ᵗʰ and included photographs some taken by Joseph Hardman. Delia also showed me an American magazine containing Hardman photos.

Delia, sadly died on the 16ᵗʰ July, 2015

Joyce Taylor (nee Fitzgerald), was interviewed at her home in Kendal – Spring-time 2013

'I don't know how my parents knew Mr Hardman because we did not live near – my father was a hairdresser so perhaps he cut Mr Hardman's hair. I would be living in Anchorite Fields, Kirkbarrow, by the time I was being taken out by Mr Hardman – so probably about 1940-45. I was born in 1933. I can't remember how long it happened, it was a period of years and I would just be told I was going out with Mr Hardman today. I can remember he used to have a taxi and always had the same driver – with auburn coloured hair. The taxi firm was on New Road, towards bottom end of Kent Street. My parents had twins a few years after I was born and the Council housed us on Kirkbarrow because the little cottage in Dockray Hall Road was not suitable at all.

I can remember sometimes my mother came with us. Mrs Hardman was nearly always there, and sometimes a sister of hers occasionally, perhaps visiting. I was only seven or eight so can't remember her name.

When, we went out, we went to the same places each year seasonally to photograph places such as the Vale of Rydal when the daffodils were there – although he did not take colour photographs as you know – always a camera, tripod and glass plates and I can picture him, a wonderful man in pants and braces and shirt – he also went to the Vale of Rydal when the leaves were beginning to drop and different places.

Joyce

He always gave my parents a copy of any photographs I was in – I kept them in an old suitcase and on moving house in my thirties when I was moving from a bigger house to a smaller house – and not knowing the value of anything then I just threw the lot away together with childhood books – things I have regretted since and left myself with no Hardman photographs at all. Then as I have grown up he has come more into the news and I have appreciated them in all sorts of ways.

He was always greeted with open arms whenever he went to certain farms. He took a lot of photos of farm workers and they are the classic ones really. I'm featured at a farm at the side of the Old Dungeon Ghyll Hotel giving the chickens or ducks handfuls of grain.

I remember when I was eighteen seeing myself in a calendar – quite a few years after it had been taken. Most weeks there were photographs of his in the Westmorland Gazette.

He very rarely just took views there were always figures in somewhere. It was always fun to go out and remembering it was wartime and rationing, he always went to places where he got a cup of coffee or something, like that and on a number of occasions he would go for afternoon tea to the Wateredge Hotel, Ambleside. I can remember he was being served, when you would get an egg ration for a week, but he used to get two boiled eggs for himself always! He had such a wonderful personality.'

Joyce then went on to say, 'I met Sylvia Deacon in Windermere Library and she gave me some photos. I was born in 1933 and Sylvia in 1925. She remembered me.'

*Nurses and babies evacuated from the North East (Newcastle)
'Just a line from Grasmere, Lake District' 15/11/39*

Daphne Rockcliff (nee Bird), at Oxenholme – 10th August 2013

I was fortunate to meet up with Daphne at her home as a result of a newspaper article I had placed in the Westmorland Gazette newspaper requesting anyone who had any knowledge of Joseph Hardman to contact me.

Daphne told me that she could not remember anything about being one of Joseph's models, or how she became one as she was very young, and was only about seven when the photographs were taken in 1940-1.

Daphne then told me about the two evacuees from South Shields who lived with them during the war at their home at Vicars Walk, Kendal, and that they had also been models. They were Florence (Florrie Bryant) and Gywneth (Patterson) and were in their teens.

'We had the girls for quite some time the whole family used to come up and visit and they came for the day.'

Daphne

58

Gwyneth Dillarstone (nee Patterson)

On trying to trace Gwyneth Patterson from South Shields I managed to find an article written by Gwyneth of her war years and was doubly fortunate to trace and contact her daughter Barbara on the 19th January, 2014.

She told me that her mother, Gwyneth had, sadly, died on the 15th December, 2011, aged 86 and her father three weeks later – they were a very devoted couple. Gwyneth had talked about being an evacuee and how later after coming back home when she was 15yrs old, she would return to the Bird family for a week's holiday.

She used to enjoy accompanying Mr Hardman and his wife out in the car – and proudly used to show the thirty or so postcard sized photographs (well-thumbed through) that Joseph had taken of her whilst out on their trips in the Lake District. Barbara went on to say how Joseph used to get extra petrol coupons and had to be careful regarding putting down weather details – as Germans could make use of this information. Gwyneth was on a photograph that was featured in a calendar they had and when their house was bombed by the Luftwaffe they managed to retrieve it. Mum was always very proud of her photographs. Barbara went on to say that St John's School, South Shields, was just a little school – so did not have many pupils

Flo & Gwyneth at Troutbeck

and that would have been the full contingent that came to Kendal. The school was knocked down; it had stood beside the church which is still there.

By good fortune, Gwyneth had heard of a project, set up by the BBC, requesting people to write down their memories of those who had lived and fought during World War 2. This project ran from June 2003 to January 2005 and Gwyneth had written down details and sent it off to the BBC, along with others, and was under the heading WW2 People's War Evacuation and was on the internet.

Here is the article that Gwyneth contributed:-

*When the war started in 1939, I was thirteen years old and attended St. Johns School in South Shields (*on the Tyne*). It was decided to evacuate all children for safety. Our school was sent to Kendal in the Lake District. As my brother David was only two years old, my mother was allowed to be evacuated as well.*

*The school children went one day and the following day we got on the train in South Shields station. The train was packed with mothers, babies and toddlers and a few older children. The toilets didn't work and there was no water to drink. It seemed to take for ever, but eventually we arrived at Kendal. Everyone was picked up by cars; we were about the last to leave the station and we were taken to a school hall (*St George's*) and given tea and buns. We then went by car to various homes where they did not want to take us in! I know I felt very upset at their refusal. The last house we went to was in Woolpack Yard, in a saw mill and joinery shop. There was a three-storey house in the yard and our hearts sank as we were given the very top room in the house, with a double bed and a cot for David. Mrs Gibson was our hostess. She had two daughters, Isabel was my age and we became friends, Mary was eleven and a mischief maker, we never got on.*

*The next day, I went to school and met all my friends and found out where they were billeted. Joan and Margaret had been out in the orphanage (*Howard Home, now Stonecross Manor Hotel*) and hated it. My mother got them moved to a better home.*

David was ill all the time we were there and after a lot of thought my mother went back home with him, but she moved me from Mrs Gibson's to a much better home with my friend, Florrie Bryant. We stayed for nearly two years with Mr and Mrs Bird and their five year old daughter Daphne.

60

My mother took David home the week before Christmas for two reasons; firstly David was ill and secondly because she was worried about my father who worked shifts on the South Shields Ferry. She was worried about him coming in from work late to a cold house with no food ready.

After mother left life in Kendal settled down to a cold winter. We had a two mile walk to school and came home for lunch every day. It seemed like we were always walking back and forwards. Eventually we were introduced to Mr and Mrs Hardman. He was a local business man and a keen photographer. He and Mrs Hardman used to call for us at the weekend in a hired car and take us around the Lake District and taking photographs which appeared in the London newspapers and the Manchester Guardian – 'Little evacuees enjoyed Lakeland scenery'. We had a wonderful time as they always took us to big hotels for our lunch and we could pick what we liked from the menu. I remember the car and of course there was very little traffic on the roads, so we saw all the Lakeland scenery.

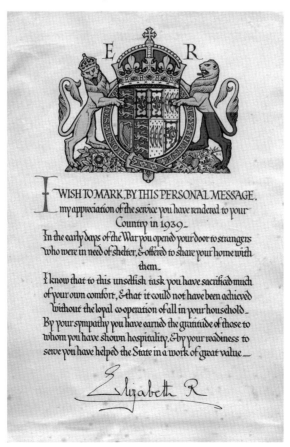

Certificate from the Queen to those who looked after the evacuees

61

In November 1940 my mother had a baby girl (my sister Janet). I was dying to see her, so when most of the people from my school came home for Christmas I came back with them. We stayed for two weeks and then returned to Kendal; thank goodness we had no air raids during that time. After a while I felt I should return home and start work. I was fifteen now and could do shorthand and typing. It was quite a shock being back home because the air raids had started again and I wasn't used to them. I started work in a solicitors' office. On the evening of 2nd October 1941 at 8pm we were bombed out. David was four and Janet just eleven months. We were lucky to escape without injury as quite a few people were killed or injured that night.'

It is interesting to note that after war was declared on 3rd September 1939, forty-four thousand Newcastle children were evacuated to places in Northumberland, Cumberland and Yorkshire.

This was because the ship building, docks, factories and steel works of the city would be a target for the enemy bombing.

But none-the-less, by 21st October 1939, eleven thousand had returned to the city.

Kendal Rush Hour in 1953

(Museum of Lakeland Life and Industry, Lakeland Arts Trust)

The first of Joseph's negatives to be scanned: two heavy horses ploughing the fields with the Howgills in the background

Chapter Seven

Digitising and bringing into the 21st Century

Sadly, out of the 50-60,000 glass plate negatives that Joseph took - the Museum of Lakeland Life and Industry in Kendal only have about 4,500 of these and nothing is known of the rest.

In 2011, the Lakeland Arts Trust was awarded nearly eight thousand pounds from the Gannett Foundation (charitable arm of Gannett Co Inc, the parent of Newsquest Media Group which owns The Westmorland Gazette of Kendal) which has enabled the negative collection to be digitised and an online photographic library created. James Arnold, the Assistant Curator was the person responsible for painstakingly getting Joseph's pictures digitised after many years in store.

He said, *'It was a nervous moment placing the first negative into the scanner and pressing the button but, thankfully a beautifully clear black and white image of two heavy horses ploughing a field appeared on the screen.'*

James Arnold

Hannah White was taken on as Project Assistant and she was to continue the digitising. She explained how Joseph would have used a view camera, inside which glass plates coated in light sensitive emulsion were placed. When exposed to the light, an image would have been captured as a permanent record within the photographic emulsion onto the plate. These are known as glass plate negatives and from them it is possible to produce black and white photographic prints. James had already scanned 1500 of the glass plate negatives, leaving 3000 remaining to complete.

At the same time she was cataloguing information about each negative recording details eg numbering, a brief description, condition and tag (key) words. This was the important information that had been sadly missing when the glass plates were originally donated to Abbot Hall in 1972. If you remember this was all the details that Edith used to write down in her little black books and Joseph used to constantly check that she had got everything.

The second part of the project was to upload the images onto a specially commissioned online library. This would allow members of the public to search through the scanned images and assist in their identification and at the same time safeguard the images. It would also provide an excellent resource for further research and enquiries regarding this valuable archive.

James went on to state, 'The beauty of putting the images into the public domain is that they are now not only sitting on a shelf in the museum's store but are being enjoyed. The information that we receive can make its way back to the catalogue to continue to build information about this irreplaceable record of Lakeland life.' This has proven very popular and many people have contacted them, including university students studying changes in weather and rural infra-structure.

For the last few years the Westmorland Gazette has put one of Joseph's pictures in the paper each week requesting details – which has proved successful. So the quest for information continues.

Chapter Eight

The re-enactment of the sheep scene coming down Allhallows Lane, Kendal.

In August 2014 after a lot of work and planning by organisers and publicity by the Westmorland Gazette, the scene was recreated of sheep coming down Allhallows Lane on their way back home from over-wintering in lowland farms. The Westmorland Gazette on Thursday, 7th August, 2014 has a large picture of Joseph Hardman's well known photograph 'Kendal Rush Hour', taken in 1953, and shows locals going about their daily business as 150 sheep were herded down Beast Banks and Allhallows Lane on their way home from over-wintering (see page 63). This would have been a scene that was a regular occurrence in those times and it was replicated at 8am on Sunday, 24th August, 2014.

Kendal's motto is 'wool is my bread' and the re-enactment was to promote the Kendal Wool Gathering and the Westmorland County Show. The sheep were going to be enclosed on Queens Road and then released with the shepherdess Alison O'Neill, a well-known Sedbergh shepherd, driving them. There were specially selected local people (related to original people or the actual person) asked to stand in exactly the same positions as those in the original picture together with vehicles.

Helen Issac, a local photographer was engaged to take this important photograph from the 1st floor window of the Town Hall which gives a clear view up Allhallows Lane. This would be where Joseph had stood with his camera, though people would have been unaware of what he was doing and would have just been going about as normal.

On the morning of Sunday, 24th August, people arrived early to position themselves to spectate – it had been well publicised. We watched the organisers busy making sure vehicles and people were being positioned exactly as they (or their relative) were on the original photograph. Farmers were busy, quietly, putting metal barriers in position. It was a bright but very cold morning – young and old were chatting and vying to find best position – there were many cameras at the ready – of both keen amateur and professionals – also Radio Cumbria and reporters. It seemed to take forever.

The Police stopped the traffic for a short time to allow proceedings to go ahead safely. The signal was given and the Kendal Rough Fell sheep came quietly down Beast Banks onto Allhallows Lane followed by Alison O'Neill and her sheepdog. Everyone went quiet trying to get 'that photograph' – there was a striking atmosphere and people were aware that it was a special moment being recreated. Everything went like clockwork and afterwards the sheep were loaded into awaiting floats down Lowther Street – they did not have to go on foot for miles as their ancestors had done. A few minutes later with many photographs taken, people were chatting excitedly about whether or not they had managed to take a good photograph. Some mentioned that their grandparents had a copy of the original photograph hanging in their halls or sitting rooms.

There were many of us trying to re-capture that famous scene, including professionals. Radio Cumbria was present recording interviews and, of course, the lady taking the all-important photograph that Joseph had taken many years before.

I am sure Joseph would have been amazed by the large number of people in attendance there, of all ages, from different backgrounds, together with the various arrays of photographic equipment being used - from the latest digital cameras and phones, to professional television cameras. Now many years later we have an updated version of 'Kendal Rush Hour' in the 21st century!

Chapter Nine

What a Picture!

Where does one start and how does one choose? I have had the good fortune of looking at hundreds of his lovely photographs and I now have the difficult task of including only a few amongst so many. So please enjoy!

Farmer Jimmy 'Whiskers' Inman threshing with a flail in a barn. He lived and farmed at Draw Well, The Howe, in the Lyth Valley, near Kendal. (Museum of Lakeland Life and Industry, Lakeland Arts Trust)

Sowing oats at Mr Moore's, Outerthwaite Farm, Flookburgh, North Lancashire. The fiddle is still used regularly, going in corners where tractors are difficult. 21/3/61.
(Cumbria Archive Centre, Kendal)

Cartmel in the 1940s. (Museum of Lakeland Life and Industry, Lakeland Arts Trust)

In February 1943 at the North of England Ploughing Championship at Skelton, near Penrith. Titled 'Stepping out to Victory'. Montgomery and Alexander, owned by Mr R Holliday, Horse and Farrier, Ellonby, won three prizes.

(Cumbria Archive Centre, Kendal)

Also in 1943 at Skelton, Mr A.W. Pearce of Loxwood, Sussex, won three prizes - one of which was for being the oldest plougher. (Cambria Archive Centre, Kendal)

In the harvest field at High Foulshaw, Gilpin Bridge, Westmorland. The tractor drawn machine cuts the wheat binds and knots it off with string in one operation. (Cumbria Archive Centre, Kendal)

Gathering in the wheat crop in Cumberland (Cumbria Archive Centre, Kendal)

Wonderful photo of traction engine bellowing out smoke belt powering harvester and sheaves being thrown in and horse and cart being loaded with straw.

(Cumbria Archive Centre, Kendal)

Threshing at Ings, near Windermere.

Jonty Wilson and two horses on a riding trip to Orton. (Museum of Lakeland Life and Industry, Lakeland Arts Trust)

Appleby Fair, 1940s.

Romany family (Cumbria Archive Centre, Kendal)

Ploughing in the snow. Old photo, possibly 1940s. The ploughman is on Westmorland border. The fells in the background are the 'Howgills' in the West Riding, on the Yorkshire border. (Cumbria Archive Centre, Kendal)

Horses and sledge are still used on the steeper of the Sedbergh slopes. (Cumbria Archive Centre, Kendal)

Saint Swithins Day at Keswick on Saturday. Heavy rains as the people were on their way to the opening meeting of the Keswick Convention. 16/7/50.

Wash and brush up at the Birketts, Yew Tree Farm, Coniston.

Glencoin, Ullswater. Going to the autumn sales.

Wives and children helping to feed clippers.
(Museum of Lakeland Life and Industry, Lakeland Arts Trust)

Dry Howe, Selside. (Museum of Lakeland Life and Industry, Lakeland Arts Trust)

Curling, at the foot of Skiddaw - near Keswick. (Museum of Lakeland Life and Industry, Lakeland Arts Trust)

Horse pulling plough, fells and lakes in background - Loweswater. (Above & Below - Museum of Lakeland Life and Industry, Lakeland Arts Trust)

81

Sea-washed turf at Sandside, Morecambe Bay - April 1942.

Cricket in hay field. (Museum of Lakeland Life and Industry, Lakeland Arts Trust)

Charcoal burning. (Museum of Lakeland Life and Industry, Lakeland Arts Trust)

Preparation for Easter sailing on Windermere. Workmen on motor yacht Teal at Lakeside, preparing for Easter. Gummers Howe snow-covered in background. 5/4/66. (Cumbria Archive Centre, Kendal)

Cars and lorries going up a snowy A6 - Shap. (Museum of Lakeland Life and Industry, Lakeland Arts Trust, above & below)

Damson time. In the Lyth Valley, 2 horses – one being fed and the other ridden bareback. (Museum of Lakeland Life and Industry, Lakeland Arts Trust)

Haymaking at Mr J. Nicolson's, Old Hall, Nibthwaite, Coniston Water, where elements have caused delay. The boat is the 'Gondola', which was launched on Coniston Water in 1860 and was in regular service until the war years. It sank two years ago and was raised in June of this year, and is owned now by Mr Adam of Walney.

(Cumbria Archive Centre, Kendal)

Man standing on back of cart, pulled by horse through ford at Crosby Garret.
(Museum of Lakeland Life and Industry, Lakeland Arts Trust)

Oxenholme Staghounds, Old Hutton. (Cumbria Archive Centre, Kendal)

The start of the Hound Trail at the Wasdale Sports, held at the foot of Gt Gable, 3000 ft. Trail is held over 10 to 12 miles along the slopes and over the mountain tops. Winner was 'Ransom' owned by Ben Pattinson (on left edge), 41 minutes 35 seconds. (Museum of Lakeland Life and Industry, Lakeland Arts Trust)

Walter Parkin, huntsman of the Lunesdale Pack, moves-off from Smardale Hall, Westmorland. A day off for the farm workers. (Cumbria Archive Centre, Kendal)

Dry stone walling is often handed down in the family. Here, Miles Capstick Jnr started early. His father is a recognised expert. Here his is receiving coaching by his grandfather. Picture at Sedbergh.
(Above & Below - Cumbria Archive Centre, Kendal)

Cutting trees.

Lunch time at Thirlmere. (Cumbria Archive Centre, Kendal)

Robert Wilson and Elizabeth Ellen Wilson, who lived in Bolton-le-Sands and fished for cockles in Morecambe Bay. The cart was pulled by Tommy, and was filled with cockles, some of which were transported by train for sale in Preston. (Museum of Lakeland Life and Industry, Lakeland Arts)

Keswick on market day. (Museum of Lakeland Life and Industry, Lakeland Arts Trust)

A daily scene at Lyth, Westmorland (Cumbria Archive Centre, Kendal)

Cycling along the shore of Windermere (Cumbria Archive Centre, Kendal)

A view of Lunesdale huntsmen on horseback, Hodge Hill Hall - Mrs Johnstone
(Museum of Lakeland Life and Industry, Lakeland Arts Trust)

Glenridding mine buildings. (Above & Below - Museum of Lakeland Life and Industry, Lakeland Arts Trust)

A typical early farming scene (Museum of Lakeland Life and Industry, Lakeland Arts Trust)

Boy sowing corn (Museum of Lakeland Life and Industry, Lakeland Arts Trust)

Ploughing, near Levens, Westmorland (Museum of Lakeland Life and Industry, Lakeland Arts Trust)

Hay-time scene with Cartmel Priory in the background (Cumbria Archive Centre, Kendal)

Chapter Ten

Summing up Joseph's Legacy and the Future

There is no doubt that we owe a huge debt of gratitude to Joseph and all that he did. He has left us with a fantastic photographic legacy of rural life and culture, in particular farming in Cumberland and Westmorland, for almost forty years from the 1930s.

It was as if it he had taken it upon himself to make it his mission in life to record everything in that era, in rural life and industry – indeed the agricultural revolution. Many people did not have cars or transport – the age of horse and cart was disappearing. He witnessed the war years – where everybody had to 'make do and mend'. The many rural crafts in the different areas, recording past-times and rural pursuits, in the countryside – he appeared to have covered every nook and cranny of our county and neighbouring counties – be it village, fell, river, woodland, lake, valley, farm – the subjects and places he covered are endless.

Joseph dedicated his life to it as long as he possibly could and judging from the photograph of Joseph and his window cleaning equipment he worked doing both jobs well into his fifties before he gave up cleaning and continued photography as long as his health held up. The last picture I have found was dated December 1966 and he died aged 79 in 1972. He obviously took pictures as long as he could – the telling time, would be financially, the costs involved, the changing times and of course inevitably his own age and health.

We all have to some extent in our lives had that window of opportunity whatever that might be and Joseph saw his, grasped it with both hands and ran with it. He surely captured that period in time to a T. There have been other photographers along the way – but he seems to have conscientiously gone about it meticulously trying to record everyday rural life, changes and developments along the years. By the 1960s he had covered and done everything possible – he had successfully filled that gap.

He was a man of the people with no airs and graces; what he had he shared, he was jovial and kind. Not many people had cameras and he generously gave the farmers a copy of what he had taken. He ventured into marketing some of his pictures into post cards and selling them to some of the small post offices in the Lake District that were popular with the early tourists. He never converted to taking colour, though he did experiment with aquatints, he just continued taking his marvellous black and white pictures.

He filled that niche in time which was fortunate for us all. He had his heyday. The world of photography as Joseph and Edith knew it was moving on and the world and countryside was changing and we were about to enter the world of computers (computer appreciation).

Of the many glass plate negatives taken the Museum of Lakeland Life and Industry, in Kendal, have about 4,500. There are also many photographs held at Kendal Library and these are used in displays and talks along with the work of other local photographers of the era. Photographs are also held at the Archives, in County Hall, Kendal. Some of the major newspapers and magazines may hold some in their own archives.

It is interesting to note that, as a result of the digitising of the glass plates and information on the computer by the Museum of Lakeland Life and Industry, that Universities are now aware of them and their importance in research such as Snow Scenes Project. Students from Nottingham study snow scenes, attempting to expand regional understanding of snow and severe winters in Britain through archival research on past extreme winters. Finding the location, taking walls and such like that remain at the scene as a reference they then take up-to-date photographs and experiment using graphic editing software which merges and blends the originals with the new digitised photographs of the location.

Upon examining some of the photographs they were struck by the continuity of buildings, walls and fences but noted the changes in land were connected to changing economics. At times showing a reduction of hedges for field boundaries, field use changed and plantations come and gone.

Joseph's photographs have also been used in a project in 2014 carried out by the Museum of Lakeland Life and Industry, to assist a small group of dementia sufferers to recover lost memories from earlier years. They were shown pictures taken by Joseph and being able to identify the locations and then going out to visit.

The Local Studies Section at Kendal Library over the years has shown displays of his work together with other local photographers of that time, at the Library or various agricultural shows. They have found that people of all ages come and look at the photographs. A few just give a passing glance, others can stand for some time, viewing the people pictured, old scenes, traditions and agricultural machinery and ask many questions. Some even find pictures of their ancestors and go away delighted.

The worry for future years is that with the rise of digital photography using a wide variety of systems and equipment, that images may no longer be stored as well as Joseph's have been. And digital images will be deleted or destroyed as equipment fails and we will not have access to these images.

So all these years later and Joseph is still very much in a lot of people's minds and indeed his pictures are being put to good use. Not only do grandparents remember him – but youngsters – his pictures are viewed on the computer, discussed, local newspaper, displayed and copies sold in the Museum of Lakeland Life and Industry, university students are studying and using them re weather, how important they are as a part of our history and indeed research our past as there is so much information to be gleaned from them.

Joseph and Edith's story does not end here and lives on today thanks to the vast legacy of nearly forty years of wonderful black and white photographs he has left us with capturing rural life and culture in Westmorland and Cumberland from the 1930s. The photographs are as crisp and clear as if they were taken yesterday. Coupled with these are the people still around who remember him and who have given freely of their time, recounting the wonderful memories they have of this quiet couple.

I am sure should Joseph and Edith be looking down they would be quietly proud of how their work is being aired and used today in the 21st century.

Herdwick sheep and shepherd crossing Ashness Bridge (Museum of Lakeland Life and Industry, Lakeland Arts Trust)

Sources

Cumbria Archives Centre, Kendal - Family Estate and Personal - Private Records Collection WD/Hd4 - Boxes 1 to 4.

Local Studies Section, Kendal Library.

Museum of Lakeland Life and Industry, Kendal.

Radcliffe Public Library.

Radcliffe Times – 6th January 1900.

Bury Registrar Office.

The Herald (Penrith) December 1951.

University of Reading – Museum of Rural Life.

Cumbria Magazine – 1953, 2002 – Bill Mitchell.

Cumbria Life – 2006 - Keith Richardson.

Cumbria Life – 2007 - Claire Sherwen.

BBC – WWII People's War Evacuation.

Charles F. Horne, National Alumni 1923.

Records of the Great War, Vol V1, ed.

British Admiralty Statement on the Zeebrugge and Ostend Raids, 22-23 April Raid 1918.

The Raid on Zeebrugge – Colin McKenzie.

National Archives Kew – War record – Royal Marine Light Infantry – 11 Sept 1917 Ref No ADM 159/179/2493 - researched by Chris Payne and Phil Bonney.

Westmorland Gazette - 20th December 2012 - Adrian Mullen.

Westmorland Gazette - 7th and 21st August 2014 - Patrick Christys.

IF YOU HAVE ENJOYED THIS BOOK YOU MAY ALSO ENJOY OTHER
BOOKS PUBLISHED BY HELM PRESS
(Not all now available - please enquire)

'A Westmorland Shepherd' His life, poems and songs

'Elephants on the Line' Tales of a Cumbrian Railwayman (1947-95)

'Dear Mr Salvin' The story of the building of a 19th century Ulverston Church

'All in a Lifetime' The story of a Dalesman as told by June Fisher

'Over the Rainbow' A collection of poems for everyone

'Hawkshead Revisited' A Walk in time through Hawkshead

'A Century of Heversham and Leasgill' A walk in time through these old
Westmorland villages

'An Old Westmorland Garage' The story behind Crabtree's of Kendal

'Ambleside Remembered' People and Places, Past and Present

'Snagging Turnips and Scaling Muck' The Women's Land Army in Westmorland

'The Windermere Ferry' History, Boats, Ferrymen and Passengers

'Kendal Green' A Georgian Wasteland Transformed

'Kendal Brown' The history of Kendal's Tobacco and Snuff Industry

'Stainton' An Old Westmorland Parish

'On and Off the Rails' The life of a Westmorland Railwayman

'Jack's Lad' The life of a Westmorland Agricultural Contractor 1953-2000

'A Year in Silverdale' Observations of natural life in and around this Lancashire Village

'From Cotton Mills to Lakeland Hills' Holiday Cottage in Lake District 1930s

'PoW to Lancashire Farmer' The remarkable life of Alec Barker

'It Were Like This Me Lass!' Kendalians tell us about life in Kendal from the 1900s

'Skip Cannon Recalls' A lifetime of Scouting in Westmorland

'Natland and Oxenholme' The story of a Westmorland Village

HELM PRESS
10 Abbey Gardens, Natland, Kendal, Cumbria LA9 7SP
E-mail: anne.bonney1@btinternet.com